Foreign Exchange (Forex)

AND

High-Yield Investment Program (HYIP)

Fraud

Commodity Futures Trading Commission (CFTC)

CONTENTS

Fraud Advisory from the CFTC: Profits Based on Hurricane Katrina

Fraud Advisory from the CFTC: Profits Based on Seasonal Demand or Other Well-known Public Information

Fraud Advisory from the CFTC: Profits from the War on Terrorism

Fraud Advisory from the CFTC: Phony Futures and Options Websites

Commodity Futures Trading Commission (CFTC) Consumer Advisory: Forex Fraud

If it sounds too good to be true, it probably is!

Foreign currency trading scams often attract customers through advertisements in local newspapers, radio promotions, or on attractive Internet sites. These advertisements may peddle high-return, low-risk investment opportunities in foreign currency trading, or even highly paid currency-trading employment opportunities. Precious metals scams often work the same way.

The CFTC urges you to be skeptical when promoters of foreign currency trading claim that their services or account management will earn high profits with minimal risks, or that employment as a currency trader will make you wealthy quickly.

CFTC's advises on Forex fraud available:

Unsafe Conditions

Forex fraudsters typically:

●Promise profits, but they don't deliver — their customers lose money instead!

●Claim most customers make money, when in fact most lose.

●Claim to be trading customers funds, when in fact they are stealing them.

●Give you phony success stories from made-up customers.

●Create fake account statements showing false trading profits.

•Claim that they have been in business for years, when in fact it is often only months.

•Claim to be solid and stable firms, until they disappear and leave customers calls unanswered.

Be Alert

If you hear this...

"You can make six-figure profits within a year."

"Forex investments are very low risk."

"You can double your money."

"Mortgage your house or use your retirement funds. My recommendations can't miss."

"You will make money whether exchange rates move up or down."

"You must invest right now or it will be too late."

...Don't Invest!

Moving Violations

In a recent period, the CFTC filed over 80 enforcement actions in federal court against hundreds of firms, owners and employees for defrauding over 23,000 customers who lost over $300 million in these forex schemes.

Many of these forex fraudsters were also criminally prosecuted and are now in jail. However, the defrauded investors rarely recovered any of the funds they lost.

Consumer Advice

●No matter what you're told, forex trading is risky.

●Don't be pressured into an immediate decision.

●Use common sense.

●Get everything in writing.

●Check with the CFTC.

●Seek advice from an accountant, lawyer or an independent 3rd party.

●Don't invest more than you can afford to lose.

●Don't mortgage your home or cash in your savings to trade forex.

Foreign Exchange Currency Fraud: CFTC/NASAA Investor Alert

Beware of Foreign Currency Trading Frauds. The advertisements seem too good to pass up. They tout high returns coupled with low risks from investments in foreign currency (forex) contracts. Sometimes they even offer lucrative employment opportunities in forex trading.

Do these deals sound too good to be true?

Unfortunately, they are, and investors need to be on guard against these scams. They may look like a new, sophisticated form of investment opportunity, but in reality they are the same old trap—financial fraud in fancy garb.

Forex trading can be legitimate for governments and large institutional investors concerned about fluctuations in international exchange rates, and it can even be appropriate for some individual investors. But the average investor should be wary when it comes to forex offers.

The Commodity Futures Trading Commission (CFTC) and the North American Securities Administrators Association (NASAA) warn that off-exchange forex trading by retail investors is at best extremely risky, and at worst, outright fraud.

What are forex contracts?

Forex contracts involve the right to buy or sell a certain amount of a foreign currency at a fixed price in U.S. dollars. Profits or losses accrue as the exchange rate of that currency fluctuates on the open market. It is extremely rare that individual traders actually see the foreign currency. Instead, they typically close out their buy or sell commitments and calculate net gains or losses based on price changes in that currency relative to the dollar over time.

Forex markets are among the most active markets in the world in terms of dollar volume. The participants include large banks, multinational corporations, governments, and speculators. Individual traders comprise a very small part of this market. Because of the volatility in the price of foreign currency, losses can accrue very rapidly, wiping out an investor's down payment in short order.

How do the scams work?

Forex scams attract customers with sophisticated-sounding offers placed in newspaper advertisements, radio promotions, or on Internet sites. Promoters often lure investors with the concept of leverage: the right to "control" a large amount of foreign currency with an initial payment representing only a fraction of the total cost. Coupled with predictions about supposedly inevitable increases in currency prices, these contracts are said to offer huge returns over a short time, with little or no downside risk.

In a typical case, investors may be assured of reaping tens of thousands of dollars in just a few weeks or months, with an initial investment of only $5,000. Often, the investor's money is never actually placed in the market through a legitimate dealer, but simply diverted—stolen—for the personal benefit of the con artists.

What are regulators doing?

The CFTC is the Federal agency with the primary responsibility for overseeing the commodities markets, including foreign currency trading. Many state securities regulators also have the right under their state laws to take action against illegal commodities investments. Sometimes the CFTC and the states work together on cases. Examples include:

•In 2005, the CFTC and the Commissioner of Corporations of the State of California sued National Investment Consultants, Inc., and others in U.S. District Court for the Northern District of California for engaging in a forex scam involving approximately $2 million in customer funds. In 2006, the Court ordered restitution and fines amounting to $3.4 million.

•Also in 2005, the CFTC and the Texas State Securities Board (TSSB) engaged in a cooperative enforcement effort against Premium Income Corp. (PIC) and its principals. The CFTC and Securities and Exchange Commission (SEC) filed an action in U.S. District Court for the Northern District of Texas and the TSSB filed an administrative action charging PIC and its principals with engaging in an illegal $11 million forex operation. To date, the federal court has found three corporate defendants liable to pay restitution of $12 million and each was assessed a fine of $37 million. The State of Texas also has obtained cease and desist orders along with various criminal indictments and convictions. PIC's president is currently incarcerated on charges stemming from his forex scam.

•In 2004, Gregory Blake Baldwin of Utah pleaded guilty to fraud after his firm,

Sunstar Funding, accepted $228,500 from 33 investors for placement into the foreign currency market. The investors' money was not placed in the foreign currency market but was used to pay some past investors and for personal expenses of Baldwin.

•In 2003, the CFTC and the State of Oregon Department of Consumer and Business Services sued Orion International, Inc., and its principals in U.S. District Court for the District of Oregon for fraudulently soliciting over $40 million to participate in a purported forex fund. Orion, and its president Russell Cline, misappropriated virtually all the customer funds. In 2006, the Court entered fines and restitution orders against the defendants totaling almost $150 million. Cline is currently incarcerated on charges stemming from his forex scam.

•In 2002, the CFTC, the SEC and the State of Utah filed an action against a company known as "4NExchange" for violations of state and Federal laws as the firm's principals illegally offered foreign currency contracts through an alleged Ponzi scheme that cost investors nearly $15 million.

What are the warning signs of fraud?

If you are solicited by a company that claims to trade foreign currencies and asks you to invest funds, you should be very careful. Watch out for the following warning signs:

1. Be wary of promises that sound too good to be true: "You can make six figure profits within a year; forex investments are very low risk; You can double your money." Get-rich-quick schemes, including those involving foreign currency trading, tend to be frauds.

2. Be skeptical about unsolicited phone calls offering investments, especially those from out-of-state salespersons or companies that are unfamiliar.

3. Be especially cautious if you have acquired a large sum of cash recently and are looking for an investment vehicle. In particular, retirees with access to their retirement funds may be attractive targets for fraudulent operators. Getting your money back once it is gone can be difficult or impossible.

4. Be wary of high-pressure efforts to convince you to send or transfer cash immediately to the firm, via overnight delivery or the Internet.

5. Be smart about the money you do put at risk. Even when purchased through the most reputable dealer, forex investments are extremely risky. If you are tempted to invest, make sure you understand these products and above all, only invest what you can afford to lose. Don't invest your rent money in a forex contract.

Investigate before you invest

Investors should make sure that anyone offering a forex investment is properly licensed and has a reputable business history. The public can obtain information about any firm or individual registered with the CFTC, including any actions taken against a registrant, through the National Futures Association (NFA) Background Affiliation Status Information Center (BASIC), available on the NFA website at:

http://www.nfa.futures.org/basicnet

You can also find out if someone is registered by calling the National Futures Association at 1-800-676-4632.

The CFTC's Division of Enforcement has established a toll-free telephone number to assist members of the public in reporting possible violations of the commodities laws. Call 866-FON-CFTC (866-366-2382). In addition, if you think that you have been a victim of a forex scam, you can report suspicious activities or information to the CFTC in the online form on the this website, or by mail addressed to the Office of Cooperative Enforcement, CFTC, 1155 21st Street, NW, Washington, D.C. 20581.

The securities regulator in your state or province also may be able to help. Visit NASAA's website at www.nasaa.org to contact your state or provincial securities regulator.

Trading Futures and Options: Protection Against Fraud

The CFTC's fraud awareness and prevention program involves:

- educating futures market users
- protecting futures market participants and
- reviewing information and complaints that market participants send to us.

The CFTC is the Federal agency that regulates the trading of commodity futures and options contracts in the United States and takes action against firms suspected of illegally or fraudulently selling commodity futures and options.

Before you trade in commodities or futures, **know** the kinds and signs of fraud and the basics of futures trading.

Protect yourself from the many types of commodities fraud that exist in today's financial markets.

Be suspicious of a promise of high profits with low risk. Scams that falsely promise high profits with low risks are everywhere. Many are targeted at specific ethnic communities using the language of that community, from New York to South Florida, from the Southwest to California, and in other areas.

Be wary of any firm or individual offering to sell you commodity futures or options on commodities, including

•precious metals, such as silver or gold

•foreign currency, such as Euros, Yen, or Deutschmarks, or

•crude oil, heating oil, unleaded gas, or agricultural products such as corn, soybeans, or cattle.

Be wary of any firm or individual offering to trade your money for you in commodity futures or options, or to pool your money with other customers.

The commodity futures and option markets are very risky and you can lose your entire investment very quickly. Anyone who claims otherwise might be breaking the law. Always ask for proof.

Watch Out For These Warning Signs of Fraud

• Get-rich-quick schemes that sound too good to be true. There's never a free lunch. Be very careful if you recently retired or came into money and you're looking for a safe investment. You could be a very attractive target for a crook. Once your money is gone, it can be impossible to get it back.

31

•Predictions or guarantees of large profits. Always get as much information as you can about a firm or individual's track record and verify that information —even if you know the people involved or they are recommended by friends or relatives. If you can't get solid information about your investment and the company, don't invest. Before you invest, always check it out with someone whose financial advice you can trust.

•Promises of little or no financial risk. Be suspicious if the firm or individual says there is little risk. Be suspicious if someone tells you that a written risk disclosure statement is only a routine formality. Written risk disclosure statements are important to read thoroughly and understand.

•Claims of trading in the "Interbank Market." If a firm claims that they will trade foreign currency for you in the interbank market, or that you should trade in the interbank market, be cautious. The term "interbank market" refers to a loose network of currency transactions negotiated between financial institutions, usually banks and investment banks, and other large companies.

•Unsolicited telephone calls about investing. Be skeptical if someone you don't know calls you about investment opportunities.

•Someone asking you to send cash immediately. Be very cautious if someone tries to convince you to send cash or transfer money to them immediately by overnight express, the Internet, mail, or any other method.

Kinds of Fraud to Watch Out For

Fraud Advisories from the CFTC provide information for you about other specific kinds of fraud.

Foreign Currency Trading (Forex)

•Foreign currency trading scams often attract customers through advertisements in local newspapers, radio promotions, or on attractive Internet sites. These advertisements may peddle high-return, low-risk investment opportunities in foreign currency trading, or even highly paid currency-trading employment opportunities. Precious metals scams often work the same way.

•The CFTC urges you to be skeptical when promoters of foreign currency trading claim that their services or account management will earn high profits with minimal risks, or that employment as a currency trader will make you wealthy quickly.

Commodity Pool Operators

•Commodity pool operators often solicit investments from friends, neighbors, co-workers, and fellow religious or social group members by using their reputations in the community or their personal relationships. In many cases, however, these investment schemes turn out to be fraudulent, and you can lose your entire investment, in many cases as a result of outright theft.

•Individuals and firms that fraudulently solicit funds from investors for commodity futures and options trading are usually not registered with the CFTC. They may operate "Ponzi" schemes in which little or none of the money sent in by investors is ever invested as promised in the commodity markets. Instead, the operator of the scam steals the funds, and creates the illusion of a successful business by using some of the money put in by later investors to pay phony "profits" to earlier investors. This tactic makes it appear to investors that the investment is actually making money, which in turn attracts additional investors. Be wary of such payouts if you do not fully understand their source.

Introducing Brokers

•Introducing brokers often use advertisements and infomercials on radio and television to promote commodity futures and options. These advertisements may claim that seasonal trends in the demand for certain commodities or well-known current events (such as a hurricane or a terror attack) create an opportunity to make big money by trading in commodity futures and options. They promise quick riches, like turning $5,000 into $20,000 in just a few months, with little risk.

Before You Trade: Know the Basics of Futures Trading

•Consider your financial experience, goals, and financial resources and know how much you can afford to lose above and beyond your initial payment.

•Understand commodity futures and option contracts and your obligations in entering into those contracts.

•Understand your exposure to risk and other aspects of trading by thoroughly reviewing the risk disclosure documents your broker is required to give you.

•Understand what it means to trade on margin: margin trading can make you responsible for losses much higher than the amount you invested.

•Know who to contact if you have a problem or question.

Registration Status and Disciplinary History: Check Out the Firm or Individual Trader

•Check registration status and disciplinary history at <u>National Futures Association</u> or call NFA at 800-676-4632

•Check online for disciplinary history with the CFTC or call us at 866-366-2382

•Contact your <u>state's securities commissioner</u>

•Contact your <u>state Attorney General's Office</u> and state banking, insurance, and securities regulators (which often have their own websites)

•Contact the <u>Better Business Bureau</u>

•Contact the <u>National Fraud Information Center</u>

•Find out if firms or counter-parties with whom you plan to trade are registered or regulated institutions or entities that are outside the CFTC's jurisdiction by checking the lists of regulated institutions on the following websites (some institutions outside the CFTC's jurisdiction do not appear on any of these lists or in any other readily available places):

•Federal Reserve Board
•Federal Financial Institutions Examination Council
•Federal Deposit Insurance Corporation
•U.S. Securities and Exchange Commission
•The Office of the Comptroller of the Currency
•Office of Thrift Supervision
•National Credit Union Association
•National Association of Securities Dealers

Report Suspicious Activities or Information

To report possible violations of commodity trading laws,

•call the CFTC's Division of Enforcement at 866-FON-CFTC (866-366-2382)

Fraud Advisory from the CFTC: Precious Metals Fraud

Beware of promises of easy profits from buying precious metals and other commodities.

Be alert to companies that sell investments in precious metals and other commodities based on sales pitches claiming that you can make a lot of money, with little risk, by purchasing metal through a financing agreement.

Sometimes these companies offer opportunities to speculate on the price movement of precious metals, or other commodities such as heating oil, without actually taking delivery of the commodity.

Over the past several years, the CFTC has taken enforcement action against wrongdoers who lured customers to purchase purported interests in precious metals without taking delivery, through various misrepresentations including claims that they would earn large profits with little risk.

Certain companies advertise on radio, television, or Internet websites, or make telephone calls, to promote the purchase of precious metals such as gold, silver, and platinum. In our experience, these advertisements, infomercials, and telephone solicitations often promise quick riches, such as the ability to double or triple your initial investment in just two or three months, with low risk.

Companies making such statements typically ask that customers pay only a small percentage of the total purchase price, and also claim that they (or another company) will purchase and store the metal.

These companies also pretend to arrange financing for the customer's metal purchase so the customer can obtain a larger profit by controlling a larger amount of metal with their relatively small down payment.

Companies often discourage customers from taking delivery of the metal and often charge a commission for the purchase transaction, a loan origination fee, an interest charge on the remaining balance (which accrues over time), and fees relating to storage and shipping of the metal they pretend to purchase for the customer. Sometimes, not all of these fees are disclosed upfront.

What's Wrong With These Sales Pitches?

The CFTC's experience is that companies making such sales pitches often:

●lie about or overstate their ability to predict prices or the direction of the metals markets;

●minimize the degree of investment risk involved in metals investments;

●fraudulently fail to disclose how much the price of metal must go up for you to break even (much less make a profit), since large finance and storage fees and commissions are deducted from customer accounts before any profits accrue;

•falsely claim to be purchasing and storing the metal when they do not; indeed such companies often discourage customers from taking delivery of the metal;

•charge phony "storage" fees for metal, when no metal is actually purchased or stored;

•charge phony "interest" fees that diminish your account equity to the point where you have to deposit additional funds with the company or have your account closed out at a total loss. The interest fees are phony because no metal has been purchased as promised, and the financing arrangement therefore is fictitious;

•fail to point out that, because you are buying on "margin" or with leverage, you will have to send the company additional funds (or sell a portion of your "metal position") if the price of the precious metals moves unfavorably.

Use Extra Care When Dealing With Foreign Companies

Sometimes companies that solicit customer investments in precious metals (or their purported storage facilities) are located outside the United States and they may not reveal that fact to you while soliciting your investment.

Ask where all companies that would handle your funds are located, where any telephone call you receive originates, where your funds will be deposited and kept, and where the metal will be stored. If possible, telephone the company.

U.S. government agencies generally have little or no regulatory authority over entities operating outside the United States. If you transfer funds to foreign firms or place funds with United States firms that are later transferred to offshore companies, it may be difficult or impossible for you to recover your money.

Storing metal offshore, particularly in countries with secrecy laws, might make it difficult for you to verify your investment.

Fraud Advisory from the CFTC: Commodity Pool Fraud

Be cautious of commodity investment opportunities that promise you large profits and little risk, even if you know the people involved.

The CFTC wants to warn you about fraudulent schemes that often involve unregistered commodity pool operators. Commodity pool operators are persons or firms that raise funds and pool them together to trade commodity futures and options. Pool operators often use their reputations or personal relationships to solicit investment money from friends, neighbors, co-workers, church members, or social groups. These investment schemes may be fraudulent and you could lose your entire investment.

The CFTC is the U.S. Federal agency that regulates the trading of commodity futures and options contracts in the United States. The CFTC has brought many enforcement actions against individuals and firms, often

49

unregistered, that offered investments in commodity pools where the invested funds were misappropriated or misused (often spent on improper expenses) and where the pool operators advertised and solicited investors based on false claims of high profits and low risk.

We urge you to be skeptical when someone tells you that their services can earn you large profits with minimal risk. Be skeptical even if a friend or relative recommends these trading opportunities or services. Investors lose millions of dollars every year in phony commodity pools, and fictional "hedge funds" trading commodity futures and options.

Before you invest, find out about the registration status, business background, and disciplinary history of the pool operator. Ask for copies of the account statements that registered trading firms provide to the pool operator. If you have suspicions, report them to the CFTC quickly.

Fraudulent Sales Pitches

Pool operators often use word of mouth referrals or emails sent among friends and relatives, members of community organizations, churches, or social groups to convince people that they can make money quickly by investing in their commodity pools.

One fraudulent pool operator even solicited investments from members of his cancer support group.

In our experience, many times these pool operators promise quick riches to investors. They might promise that they can double or triple your investment in months with very little risk. Be very careful if the pool operator claims special trading expertise, a unique understanding of market trends, or claims to have a record of profitable trading. These claims by unregistered pool operators often turn out to be false.

Always be skeptical of such sales pitches even if you know the person involved. Ask the same questions and investigate what they tell you just as you would if the person was a total stranger. If you are not satisfied with the information you receive, be safe: don't invest. If you do invest, invest only the amount of money that you easily can afford to lose.

Ponzi Schemes

Individuals and firms fraudulently soliciting funds for commodity futures and options trading usually are not registered with the CFTC. They may operate Ponzi schemes. In a Ponzi scheme, little or none of investors' money is ever invested in the commodity markets as promised. Instead, the operator of this kind of scam steals the money.

Sometimes such an operator creates the illusion of a successful business by paying phony profits to early investors with some of the money the operator receives from later investors. This tactic can make it appear that the scheme is making money and attract more investors. Be very careful of such payouts if you don't understand where the money is coming from.

Operators of these scams often do not send account statements to their investors and sometimes the operators send phony account statements which falsely indicate that trading is going on and that the investor has made a profit.

Ponzi schemes are usually discovered when investors decide to withdraw their money and discover that there isn't enough money to cover their investment.

Investors can find it is expensive and difficult or even impossible to recover money lost in Ponzi schemes.

Before You Invest

You should know that certain pool operators are not required to register, including operators of small pools with 15 or fewer investors whose total trading capital equals $400,000 or less, or pool operators who receive no compensation.

These small pool operators are required to notify investors, the CFTC, and NFA that they are operating without registration.

- Ask to see the pool's disclosure documents and performance history.

- Ask the pool operator to give you account statements that the pool

53

receives from the registered firms through which the pool trades.

• Ask about all fees and commissions charged by the pool operator. Compare these fees and commissions to those of registered pool operators.

Fraud Advisory from the CFTC: Commodity Trading Systems Sold on the Internet

Beware of websites selling commodity trading systems that guarantee high profits with minimal risks.

The CFTC has seen an increase in the number of Internet websites fraudulently promoting commodity trading systems and advisory services. These websites falsely claim, among other things, that advertised performance results are based on real trading when, in fact, the results are based on hypothetical trading.

No trading system can guarantee profits! The CFTC urges you to be skeptical when promoters of trading systems and advisory services claim that their products and services will earn high profits with minimal risks. Always remember that whether or not a trading system is used, commodity futures and options are typically high-risk endeavors.

Be warned that systems which trigger frequent trading signals as part of a day trading strategy can result in substantial commissions and fees.

What Are Commodity Trading Systems?

Commodity trading systems typically are computerized programs that signal members of the public when to buy and sell commodity futures and options contracts. Systems produce buy and sell signals based on mathematical formulas and are typically based on technical analysis of trading data (trading volume and prices), as opposed to fundamental analysis (analysis of economic factors such as supply and demand).

Trading systems that are based on technical analysis attempt to predict future price movements based on historical prices, price relationships, and price trends.

Hypothetical Trading Results Can Be Unreliable

Many trading system promoters advertise their systems by reporting hypothetical trading results.

Hypothetical trading results typically are based on trading simulations using historical price data or simulated "real time" computer trading.

To obtain these results, trading system promoters typically pretend that they traded futures contracts at market prices that occurred some time in the past. They then calculate the trading results that these purported trades would have achieved had they been placed, based on actual historical prices. These results often show impressive trading results and large net profits with only a few, small margin calls.

Limitations of Hypothetical Trading Results

•Hypothetical results do not reflect the results of any actual trading whether they are based on historical data or simulated "real time" trading. In other words, there is no actual futures account, no actual investment, no actual trading, and no actual profits. The hypothetical results are purely the product of simulation.

•20/20 hindsight with historical results: since the trading systems that produced the results were not actually traded under real market conditions, the purported results fail to take into account market circumstances that affect traders and their decision-making process, such as anticipated news events that could have an impact on the supply, demand, or price of the commodity.

•Real-time is not real: when marketing trading systems, some promoters claim that their systems have performed successfully in "Real-time Trading." This means only that the system has been tested using a live data-feed, rather than being tested using historical market data.

Remember though that in real-time trading, no trades have actually been placed in the market. Performance results based on real-time trading are merely another form of hypothetical results, with the same limitations.

•Financial limitations: hypothetical results may not adequately take into account the ability of a trader to absorb trading losses or to meet margin calls. Trading systems assume that the trader can withstand all losses generated by the system and can meet resulting margin calls.

It is much easier to absorb a trading loss on paper (hypothetically) than to do so in reality. Many traders find it unacceptable to sustain several consecutive trading losses and/or margin calls. Moreover, in an actual trading environment, a trader's financial condition may change over time and affect his or her ability to continue following a trading system.

•Not tested under real market conditions: hypothetical trading results assume that futures contracts have been bought and sold at specific prices. Since these assumptions have not been subjected to actual market conditions, they may overestimate or underestimate the performance of a system.

Some market conditions may make it impossible to execute a trade; for instance, many systems assume that stop-loss orders will be executed at their stop price. Under actual market conditions a stop-loss order might be executed at a better or worse price, or not be executed at all.

Actual market conditions include bid/ask spreads which might not be reflected in the prices used in hypothetical trading.

Moreover, the actual execution of a trade could impact the price paid, especially in less liquid or illiquid markets.

●Possible rigging of results: you should be alert to the possibility that the system promoter manufactured results by selecting historical trades that would have yielded the greatest returns.

●Trading and system costs: profit claims of promoters may fail to take into consideration the cost of purchasing or leasing a trading system. While the prices of systems vary, many are sold for thousands of dollars and most of these systems require that the user obtain a data feed from a vendor.

System promoters may also fail to take into consideration the impact on profits of commissions and fees charged by brokers in connection with futures and options trading. Such commissions can have a substantial effect on profitability, particularly when the system generates frequent trading signals.

A user should take all of these costs into account because they raise the break-even point in trading.

Because of all these limitations of hypothetical trading results, CFTC rules require that the presentation of hypothetical trading results be accompanied by a specific cautionary statement warning of the inherent limitations of these results.

If you are considering trading commodity futures or options, you should educate yourself about futures and options and be aware that you may lose large sums of money.

Is a Futures/Options Trading System Right For You?

●Do you have the financial ability to sustain trading losses and meet margin calls? When trading futures contracts on margin, you risk losing much more money than the initial margin amount. If the market moves against you, you may be required to pay additional funds. The use of margin creates potentially large exposures to loss.

●Can you lose your entire investment and more without a change in your lifestyle?

●Do the trading results sound too good to be true?

●Are the advertised trading results based on actual trading or "hypothetical" trading?

●Has any trader used the system in actual trading? If so, how has the trader fared?

●Will the system promoter provide you with independent verification of the claimed trading results?

●What is the total cost of the system?

●Have you factored into your purchasing

decision the impact of commissions and fees that can result from frequent trading?

•What are the additional costs of the system (data feed, etc.)?

•What is the status of the system promoter? Not all system promoters are required to be members of the National Futures Association or registered with the CFTC. Check their registration and disciplinary status with the CFTC and the NFA.

Fraud Advisory from the CFTC: Profits Based on Hurricane Katrina

Beware of claims that the damage caused by Hurricane Katrina will increase the profitability of trading in crude oil, unleaded gasoline, heating oil, natural gas, or other commodity futures or options.

Hurricane Katrina caused extensive damage to regions of this country on the coast of the Gulf of Mexico, including New Orleans and coastal Mississippi and Alabama. Besides causing great hardship among residents of this region, the hurricane caused damage to property, including oil drilling stations and refineries located in and around the Gulf of Mexico.

The public should be advised that whatever effect these events might have on the price of physical commodities, the occurrence of such well-known events do not necessarily increase the likelihood of making profits in commodity futures or options trades that are based on these energy products or limit the risk in such trades.

Any claims made of potential profits from trading in futures or options on energy products or other commodities based on the effects of Hurricane Katrina are probably fraudulent.

The Sales Pitch

Commodity brokerage firms and brokers often use telephone calls, email messages, and mass email or spam, along with Internet advertisements, and television or radio ads, to interest members of the public in trading commodity futures and options. These brokers are prohibited by the Federal commodities laws from overstating the profitability of futures trading, understating risks, and falsifying performance history.

Brokers violate this prohibition by claiming that customers can profit based upon well-known events, such as seasonal changes in climate, natural disasters, or global conflict. Such pitches are misleading because they are meant to suggest that the broker has special information that gives him or her an edge in executing a customer's trades. That is false. It is true that increases in demand or limitations in supply of a particular commodity might affect the commodity's price. However, when such changes are already known or anticipated by the market, they will not necessarily affect the value of a futures or option position on those commodities. This is because traders in the markets have already factored this information into the price.

For example, the public, and market professionals in particular, are already aware that Hurricane Katrina has had a significant effect upon the supply of energy products such as crude oil, unleaded gas, and heating oil. These professional traders and investors who pay close attention to global economic and political factors that might affect the price of the futures and options that they trade, quickly take into account new information concerning the possibility that future supplies of these products may be disrupted. As a result, the prices of futures and options already reflect this possibility.

In addition, claims that the risk of purchasing commodity futures and options can be predetermined or fixed are misleading. Purchasers of commodity futures or options contracts can lose every penny given to a broker and, because futures contracts are "leveraged" or "margined," customers may be liable for losses in excess of their initial deposits.

The CFTC's Division of Enforcement is on the lookout for Katrina-related commodities scams and will vigorously prosecute those who attempt to take advantage of this tragedy to defraud members of the public.

Investors who believe they may have been targets of such schemes should forward suspicious solicitations to the Department of Justice's Hurricane Katrina Fraud Task Force on any potential prosecutions of such violations.

Fraud Advisory from the CFTC: Profits Based on Seasonal Demand or Other Well-known Public Information

Beware of promises of easy profits from commodity futures and options based on seasonal demand and other well-known public information.

The CFTC urges you to be alert to possible fraudulent claims that you can profit on commodity futures or options trading as a result of changes in the prices of physical commodities based on seasonal weather patterns or other well-known events.

For example, it is well known that the prices of energy commodities, such as heating oil, natural gas, and gasoline, fluctuate in response to changes in the seasons. These normal fluctuations, however, are well known by traders in the futures and options markets and already reflected in their prices.

Investing in futures and options markets is not like investing in the physical commodity itself. Just because the price you pay for heating oil or natural gas is rising does not mean that the price of heating oil or natural gas futures and options prices will also rise! As a result, there is little if any possibility to profit in these markets based on such information.

When salespeople call you claiming to be able to profit from predicted price movements based on well-publicized events such as political unrest, published reports, weather events, and market disruptions, their claims are most likely fraudulent. Futures and options markets adjust very quickly to news events and announcements, and by the time salespeople come calling, the opportunity to profit from such news is gone. In addition, beware of claims that the risk of loss can be limited; in fact, because futures contracts are "leveraged" or "margined," futures investors can lose more, and sometimes substantially more, than their initial deposit.

The CFTC urges members of the public to report any suspicious claims about energy commodity sales pitches based on seasonal demand patterns or other well-known events by calling our toll-free line at 866-FON-

CFTC (800-366-2382) or by emailing us at
questions@cftc.gov.

The Sales Pitch

The solicitation of commodity futures and
options occurs in all media, including radio,
television, print advertisements, Internet
promotions, and spam email.

You might also receive a "cold call" from a
commodity broker who obtained your name
from a list. Brokers often make repeated
phone calls to people and aggressively urge
them to open an account and send in money
immediately to take advantage of a
particular trend or event in the market.

If you see such solicitations or receive such a
call, be alert and careful if the following
types of representations are made:

> •It won't be long before cold weather is
> here. Heating oil (or natural gas)
> inventories are down and demand is
> going up!
> •You can turn $5,000 into $20,000 or
> more with just a ten-cent move in prices!
> •The situation in the Middle East has
> disrupted global oil supplies, and so

prices are bound to rise!

- We can protect your investment to limit any losses!
- You need to act quickly to seize this "can't miss" opportunity!
- You can't lose money trading options!

These pitches are all fraudulent because, in one way or another, they make unjustified profit claims or improperly minimize risk.

Fraud Advisory from the CFTC: Profits from the War on Terrorism

Beware of promises of profits from commodity futures and options trading based on the events of September 11, 2001 and other public information relating to the war on terrorism.

Be alert to solicitations for transactions in commodity futures or options contracts based on claims that you can make a lot of money with little risk by trading in commodities affected by well-known current events, such as the attacks of September 11, 2001 and the war on terrorism.

The Sales Pitch

Companies often use telephone call solicitations, email messages, Internet advertisements, websites, Internet chat room discussions, or radio and television advertisements and infomercials to promote commodity futures and options trading.

The CFTC is aware of solicitations claiming that changes in the market because of the September 11 attacks and other world events have created an opportunity to make big money by trading in commodity futures and options.

Solicitations may promise quick riches, such as turning $5,000 into $20,000 in just a few months with predetermined risk. We are aware of pitches that a purchase of futures or options in crude oil will be profitable because unrest in oil producing countries will drive up the price of this commodity.

These sales pitches are false: increases in the demand for commodities due to world events do not necessarily result in the increase in the value of an option or futures contracts. The market has already factored such demand into the price of futures and options. Markets respond immediately to new information, within a few minutes or hours. The prices of commodity options and futures contracts already take into account all known or predictable market conditions.

Claims that the risk of purchasing commodity futures and options can be predetermined or fixed are misleading. Purchasers of commodity option contracts can lose every penny and because futures contracts are leveraged or margined, customers may be liable for losses in excess of their initial deposits.

Fraud Advisory from the CFTC: Phony Futures and Options Websites

Beware of websites claiming to be the U.S. Federal regulator of futures and options trading, or to be a Federally-regulated entity.

The CFTC has seen an increase in the number of Internet websites fraudulently promoting commodity trading systems and advisory services. These websites falsely claim, among other things, that advertised performance results are based on real trading when, in fact, the results are based on hypothetical trading.

No trading system can guarantee profits! The CFTC urges you to be skeptical when promoters of trading systems and advisory services claim that their products and services will earn high profits with minimal risks. Always remember that whether or not a trading system is used, commodity futures and options are typically high-risk endeavors.

Be warned that systems which trigger frequent trading signals as part of a day trading strategy can result in substantial commissions and fees.

How to Recognize a Phony Futures and Options Website

The scams all appear to operate in a similar fashion. A fraudulent website claiming to be a registered commodity broker solicits potential customers to invest in futures or options. The website also directs the potential customer to another fraudulent website claiming to be the Federal agency responsible for the oversight of the U.S. commodity markets. Once the customer agrees to invest, the broker directs the customer to open an account with a fictitious exchange, which falsely claims to be regulated by the United States government. The fictitious exchange then directs the customer to wire funds to a bank account for trading. Customers are led to believe that they have opened online trading accounts with the exchange when, in fact, their funds have been misappropriated.

The websites are slick and professional looking, and the scams are particularly convincing because they appear to offer investors the assurances of industry and U.S. Federal government oversight. The websites even go so far as to allow potential investors to search regulator databases for registration status and to file complaints.

The CFTC warns investors to do independent research before sending funds to a commodity firm. The official websites for the CFTC, the National Futures Association (the self-regulatory organization for the U.S. commodity industry), and the International Organization of Securities Commissions are:

•Commodity Futures Trading Commission (CFTC).

•National Futures Association (NFA). The Federal commodities laws require that virtually every commodity firm doing business with the U.S. public must be a member of the National Futures Association. You'll find information on how the NFA registers and governs its member firms on its website at http://www.nfa.futures.org/. You can also check registration status of NFA member firms at the NFA website.

•International Organization of Securities Commissions (IOSCO). You'll find a list of international regulators on the International Organization of Securities Commissions website at http://www.iosco.org/.

Recommended Readings

- Siddhartha by Hermann Hesse, www.bnpublishing.net

- The Anatomy of Success, Nicolas Darvas, www.bnpublishing.net

- The Dale Carnegie Course on Effective Speaking, Personality Development, and the Art of How to Win Friends & Influence People, Dale Carnegie, www.bnpublishing.net

- The Law of Success In Sixteen Lessons by Napoleon Hill (Complete, Unabridged), Napoleon Hill, www.bnpublishing.net

- It Works, R. H. Jarrett, www.bnpublishing.net

- The Art of Public Speaking (Audio CD), Dale Carnegie, wwww.bnpublishing.net

• The Success System That Never Fails (Audio CD), W. Clement Stone, www.bnpublishing.net

BN Publishing
Improving People's Life
www.bnpublishing.net

www.ingramcontent.com/pod-product-compliance
Lightning Source LLC
Chambersburg PA
CBHW032014190326
41520CB00007B/470